Long ago, there were some very strange animals. They were called dinosaurs.

Brachiosaurus

Here are some more.

Stegosaurus

Triceratops

Dinosaurs lived so long ago that no one has ever seen one alive.

We can learn about them by finding fossils like these.

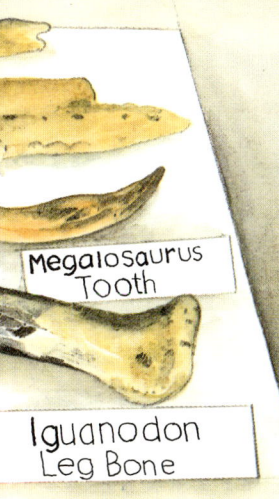

Megalosaurus Tooth

Iguanodon Leg Bone

By putting fossils together like a jigsaw, we can see what dinosaurs looked like.

We are not sure why the dinosaurs died out and became extinct.

But we can guess.

Perhaps a meteor crashed into the Earth?

Perhaps the weather changed?

Scolosaurus

Perhaps the land changed?

Iguanodon

Perhaps there was another reason?

7

Here are some other animals which became extinct.

Dodo

Giant sloth

We know more about them because they died out in the last 200 years.

Many of these animals became extinct because people hunted them.

Tasmanian wolf

Mexican silver grizzly

They are gone forever.

Today, some more animals are nearly extinct.

Bald eagle

Gorilla

Sea otter

Dormouse

Crested newt

We have to protect them, because people <u>still</u> hunt them or destroy their homes.

Tiger

Whale

Rhinoceros

Different plants and animals need different homes to live in.

If we destroy their homes . . .

. . . the plants and animals die.

One of these animals is extinct. Which one is it?

The other animals are alive today. What are they? Where might they live?

15

What types of plants, insects, birds and animals might live here?